Fish

Rod Theodorou

Heinemann Library
Des Plaines, Illinois

© 2000 Reed Educational & Professional Publishing
Published by Heinemann Library,
an imprint of Reed Educational & Professional Publishing,
1350 East Touhy Avenue, Suite 240 West
Des Plaines, IL 60018

Customer Service 1-888-454-2279

Text designed by Celia Floyd
Illustrations by Alan Fraser
Printed in Hong Kong/China

04 03 02 01 00
10 9 8 7 6 5 4 3 2 1

The Library of Congress has cataloged the hardcover version of this book as follows:
Library of Congress Cataloging-in-Publication Data
Theodorou, Rod.
      Fish / Rod Theodorou.
          p. cm. – (Animal babies)
      Includes bibliographical references and index.
      Summary: Introduces the birth, development, care, feeding, and characteristics of baby fish.
      ISBN 1-57572-882-6 (lib. bdg.)
      1. Fishes—Infancy—Juvenile literature. 2. Parental behavior in animals—Juvenile literature. [1. Fishes. 2. Animals—Infancy. 3. Parental behavior in animals.] I. Title. II. Series: Animal babies (Des Plaines, Ill.)
      QL639.25.T48 1999
      597.13′9—dc21   99-18055
                                                                    CIP
Paperback ISBN 1-57572-542-8

Acknowledgments
The Publishers would like to thank the following for permission to reproduce photographs:
Ardea London Ltd., p. 13; BBC/Jeff Foott, p. 15; Bruce Coleman/Pacific Stock, p. 7; Charles & Sandra Hood, p. 16; Jane Burton, pp. 17, 22; FLPA/Steve McCutcheon, p. 9; NHPA/Norbert Wu, p. 12; OSF/Keith Ringland, p. 6; David Thompson, p. 8; David B. Fleetham, p. 10; Zig Leszczynski, p. 11; Mark Deeble & Victoria Stone, p. 14; Rudie Kuiter, p. 20; Peter Parks, p. 23; Jeff Foott, p. 24; Rodger Jackman, p. 25; Planet Earth/Peter Scoones, p. 21; Tony Stone/Fred Bavendam, p. 5; Marc Chamberlain, p. 19.

Cover photo: Oxford Scientific Films/M. Deeble,V. Stone

Some words in this book are in bold, **like this**. You can find out what they mean by looking in the glossary.

Contents

Introduction

There are many different kinds of animals. All animals have babies. They take care of their babies in different ways.

These are the six main animal groups.

Mammal   Bird   Reptile

Amphibian   Fish   Insect

This book is about fish. Fish live in ponds, lakes, rivers, and seas all over the world. There are lots of different kinds of fish.

The whale shark is the biggest fish in the world. An adult can be as long as two school buses!

What Is a Fish?

All fish:
- live in water
- breathe **oxygen** with their **gills**
- swim using their **fins**

Salmon

fins

gills under
gill cover

scales

tail fin

6

Most fish:
- have hard **scales** on their body
- **hatch** from eggs **laid** by females

Eels are fish, but most do not have scales.
Their bodies are soft and smooth.

Making a Nest

Most fish do not make nests. They **lay** their eggs in the water and swim away. Some fish make a nest for their eggs. The nest keeps the eggs safe.

Sticklebacks make a little cave out of weeds on the **riverbed**.

8

Fish make their nests at the bottoms of rivers or on the **seabed**. They scoop out holes in the sand with their bodies. Some even push weeds into their nests.

This female salmon digs a nest and then covers her eggs with gravel to keep them safe.

Protecting the Nest

Some fish stay close to their nests and guard their eggs or baby fish from **predators**. They attack any other animal that comes near the nest.

This triggerfish will attack anything that comes near his eggs—even divers!

Female fish **lay** the eggs, but it is often the male fish that takes care of them. He may go for days without food just to **protect** the eggs.

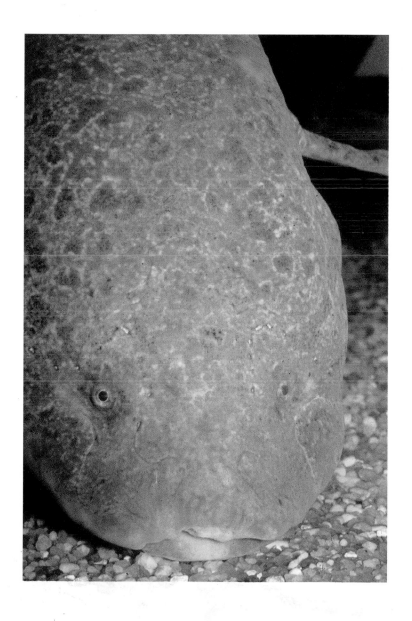

The huge African lungfish protects his nest. A lungfish can be longer than your bed!

Laying Eggs

Most fish **lay** thousands or even millions of eggs. The eggs are usually tiny and round. They do not have hard shells and are easily eaten by other animals.

When this ocean sunfish grows up, it will be able to lay over five million eggs at once.

Other fish lay hard egg cases shaped like a purse. The egg case has a curly leg at each corner that hooks onto seaweed. The eggs stay there until the babies **hatch**.

A baby dogfish shark grows inside an egg case.

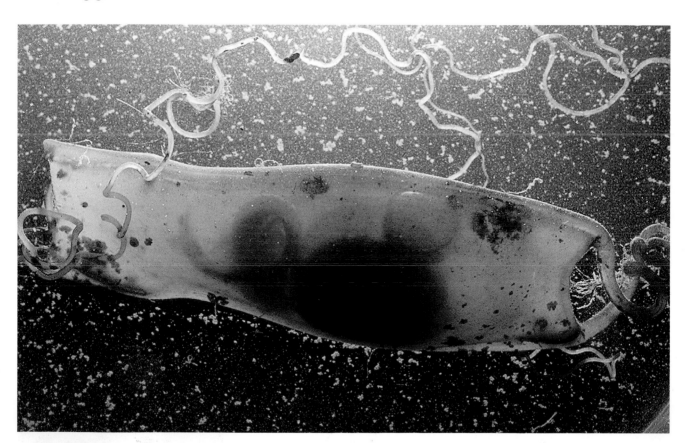

Fish Fry

When baby fish **hatch** from eggs, they are called **fry** or larva. They are often tiny—only as long as your fingernail. They do not look much like their parents, yet.

Baby fish like these emperor cichlid fry are very hard for **predators** to spot.

Some fry have a bag growing under their stomachs called a **yolk sac**. The fry do not need to look for food. They can live for weeks off the food in their yolk sacs.

This salmon fry stays hidden in gravel for weeks, living off its yolk sac.

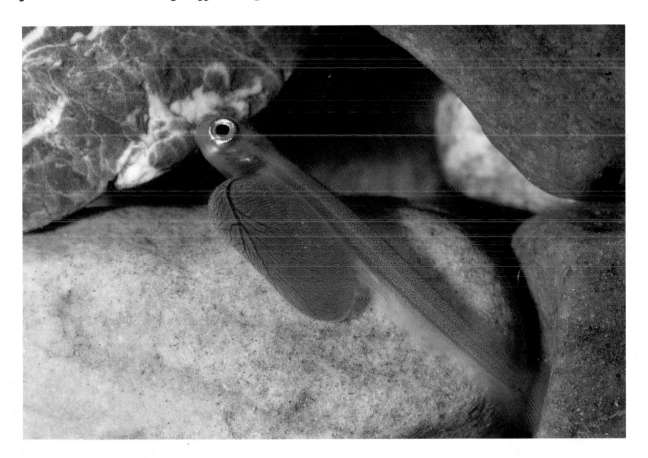

Staying Safe

When millions of fish eggs **hatch** into millions of fish **fry**, they attract lots of **predators**. Other fish, shrimps, crabs, and jellyfish eat huge numbers of fry.

This Dover sole has attacked a fish fry.

Fish fry try to stay hidden from predators.
Some hide on the **seabed** among rocks or weeds.
Others swim next to floating weeds or pieces of
wood at the surface.

*These red devil fry are hiding among rocks
on the seabed.*

Live Birth

Some sharks and other fish do not **lay** eggs. The babies grow inside their mothers and are born live. The babies are born strong and ready to catch their own food.

A baby nurse shark looks just like its mother.

Fish that give birth to live babies only have a few babies at a time. Their babies are much harder for **predators** to catch and eat than tiny fish **fry**.

Stingrays give birth to live babies.

Taking Care of Baby

Most fish do not take care of their babies. A few kinds of fish do stay close to their babies and **protect** them.

Male seahorses have a special **pouch** where the female **lays** her eggs. The babies **hatch** out from the pouch and dash back inside if they are in danger.

Some kinds of fish take care of their **fry** in their mouths! They suck up their eggs and fry and keep them safe in their mouths.

If they are in danger, these cichlid fry swim into their mothers' mouths.

Finding Food

As fish **fry** grow up their **yolk sacs** disappear, and they have to find their own food. They feed on **plankton** and other tiny water creatures.

These jewel cichlid fry are looking for food on the **seabed**.

This is a
shoal of
young fry
on the Great
Barrier Reef.

When they are not looking for food, young fish often swim together in large groups called schools or shoals. They are safer in a school if a **predator** comes near.

Amazing Journeys

Some fish do not spend all their lives in the same place. Instead, they **migrate** long distances.

Salmon **fry hatch** in rivers, where they live for two years. Then they swim down to the sea. When they are older, they swim back up the river to **breed**.

Migrating fish may take two or three years to reach the sea or river where they breed. After they **lay** their eggs, they usually die.

These young eels swim across the ocean to live in rivers. Years later they swim back to the sea to breed.

Growing Up

This is how a baby nurse shark is born.
The baby shark looks a lot like its mother.

Growth of a grey nurse shark

1 The baby shark grows inside its mother.

2 The baby is born live.

3 The baby swims off to find fish, crabs, or shrimp to eat.

This is how a sole (called a flatfish) **hatches** and grows up. The sole **fry** does not look much like its mother.

Growth of a European sole

1 The adult female **lays** about half a million eggs.

2 Tiny fish fry hatch out of the eggs. Their bodies are not flat like their mother's.

3 Soon the fry start to look more like their mother. The body becomes flatter. One eye moves from one side of the head to the other side.

4 After six weeks the fry look like their mother.

Fish and Other Animals

		Fish
What they look like:	Bones inside body	all
	Number of legs	none
	Hair on body	none
	Scaly skin	most
	Wings	none
	Feathers	none
Where they live:	Live on land	none
	Live in water	all
How they are born:	Grow babies inside body	some
	Lay eggs	most
How babies get food:	Get milk from mother	none
	Parents bring food	none

Amphibians	Insects	Reptiles	Birds	Mammals
all	none	all	all	all
4 or none	6	4 or none	2	2 or 4
none	all	none	none	all
none	none	all	none	few
none	most	none	all	some
none	none	none	all	none
most	most	most	all	most
some	some	some	none	some
few	some	some	none	most
most	most	most	all	few
none	none	none	none	all
none	none	none	most	most

Glossary

breed   a male and a female come together to make babies

fin   flat part of a fish's body that helps it swim or turn

fry   very small, young fish

gill   part of a fish's body that takes **oxygen** from water to help it breathe

hatch   to be born from an egg

lay   when an egg comes out of a female fish's body

migrate   to move from one place to another each year

oxygen   gas that all animals and plants need to breathe in order to live

plankton   tiny animals and plants that live in the sea

pouch   pocket of skin on the stomach of some animals in which their babies grow

predator   animal that hunts and kills other animals for food

protect   to keep safe

riverbed   ground at the bottom of a river

scale   small, flat, piece of hard skin on a fish's body

seabed   ground at the bottom of the sea

yolk sac   bag of food that is part of some baby fish and that they can eat after they are born

More Books to Read

Holmes, Kevin J. *Sharks*. Danbury, Conn.: Children's Press, 1997.

Lovett, Sarah. *Extremely Weird Fishes*. Jackson, Tenn.: Davidson Titles, Incorporated, 1997.

Robinson, Claire. *Shark*. Des Plaines, Ill.: Heinemann Library, 1999.

Seward, Homer. *Eels*. Vero Beach, Fla.: Rourke Press, Incorporated, 1998.

—. *Frightening Fish*. Vero Beach, Fla.: Rourke Press, Incorporated, 1998.

Telford, Carole, and Rod Theodorou. *Shark and Dolphin*. Crystal Lake, Ill.: Rigby Interactive Library, 1997.

Index